CH00407971

Memorise
Equations
for GCSE Physics

for all you young people, who find Physics a challenge, but try your best anyway.

Subscribe to GorillaPhysics on YouTube and go to gorillaphysics.com for a full list of videos organised by GCSE and A Level topic.

Published by GorillaPhysics in the UK

ISBN-13: 978-1984954589

2018

This book is intended to help memorise the equations for GCSE Physics. The best way to memorise them is to use them!

For each page there are three questions, the first is using the equation as it is, the second is a rearrangement, third is another rearrangement with at least one unit conversion.

I deliberately haven't given the working for each question, just the answer, so that you can think through the problem and then check you've done the working correctly. I've deliberately left the maths simple enough to do in your head so that you can quickly work through the problems, hopefully that equation will eventually seep into that permanent area of your brain where all your song lyrics and film quotes are kept!

Use this book instead of flash cards! So don't just go through it once and then leave it! It's meant to be flipped through time and time again until you know the equations and their units by heart!

One more thing, about algebra. Algebra is a short cut, it saves you time and makes your life easier. As examiners we understand this algebra, if you use the correct terms, we know what you mean. You can use the quantity names if you feel more comfortable, but I suggest you embrace the algebra… there's less of it to remember.

At the end there are some of the really challenging questions where you will need to use two equations to solve the problem. For this you'll need to know the equations fluently! Often you'll be able to start solving these by thinking "what *can* I calculate from the data I've been given." Usually even if you can only do one step of these two step calculations you'll pick up half the marks so that's a great start!

On you go! I really hope this book helps!

List of Equations and Exam Boards

T = triple only   H = higher tier   X = not in specification

Equation	AQA	Edexcel	OCR A	OCR B	Eduqas
$\rho = \dfrac{m}{V}$	✓	✓	✓	✓	✓
$s = vt$	✓	✓	✓	✓	✓
$a = \dfrac{\Delta v}{t}$	✓	✓	✓	✓	✓
$E_k = \dfrac{1}{2}mv^2$	✓	✓	✓	✓	✓
$\Sigma F = ma$	✓	✓	✓	✓	✓
$p = mv$	H	H	H	H	H
$W = F\Delta s$	✓	✓	✓	✓	✓
$P = \dfrac{W}{t}$	✓	✓	✓	✓	✓

Equation	AQA	Edexcel	OCR A	OCR B	Eduqas
$F = k\Delta x$	✓	✓	✓	✓	✓
$W = mg$	✓	✓	✓	✓	✓
$E_p = mgh$	✓	✓	✓	✓	✓
$P = \dfrac{F}{A}$	T	T	T	T	T
$M = Fd$	T	T	T	T	T
$Q = It$	✓	✓	✓	✓	✓
$V = IR$	✓	✓	✓	✓	✓
$E = QV$	✓	✓	✓	✓	✓
$P = IV$	✓	✓	✓	✓	✓
$P = I^2R$	✓	✓	✓	✓	✓

Equation	AQA	Edexcel	OCR A	OCR B	Eduqas
$\Delta E = Pt$	✓	✓	✓	✓	✓
$v = f\lambda$	✓	✓	✓	✓	✓
$T = \dfrac{1}{f}$	✓	X	X	X	✓
$E_f = \dfrac{\Delta E_u}{\Delta E_T}$	✓	✓	✓	✓	✓
$E_f = \dfrac{P_u}{P_T}$	✓	X	X	X	X
$\Delta E = mc\Delta T$	✓	✓	✓	✓	✓
$E = mL$	✓	✓	✓	✓	✓
$E = VIt$	X	✓	X	X	X
$PV = k$	T	T	T	T	T
$P = h\rho g$	HT	HT	HT	HT	HT

Equation	AQA	Edexcel	OCR A	OCR B	Eduqas
$v^2 = u^2 + 2as$	✓	✓	✓	✓	✓
$v = u + at$	X	X	X	X	✓
$s = \frac{1}{2}(u + v)t$	X	X	X	X	✓
$s = ut + \frac{1}{2}at^2$	X	X	X	X	H
$E_{el} = \frac{1}{2}k\Delta x^2$	✓	✓	✓	✓	✓
$M = \frac{h_i}{h_o}$	T	X	X	X	X
$F = BIl$	H	H	H	H	H
$\frac{V_p}{V_s} = \frac{N_p}{N_s}$	HT	HT	HT	HT	HT
$V_p I_p = V_s I_s$	H	✓	✓	✓	✓
$\Sigma F = \frac{\Delta p}{t}$	HT	H	X	H	X

Prefixes and Multipliers

You need to know and be able to use these unit prefixes. Pay attention to the units that are given with each equation in this book; unless otherwise stated you'll need to convert to those units before you do the calculation! The easiest way to do this is to remember the standard form multiplier for each prefix and use the $\times 10^x$ button on your calculator to input the numbers.

prefix	name	multiplier
T	tera	$\times 10^{12}$
G	giga	$\times 10^{9}$
M	mega	$\times 10^{6}$
k	Kilo	$\times 10^{3}$
d	deci	$\times 10^{-1}$
c	centi	$\times 10^{-2}$
m	milli	$\times 10^{-3}$
μ	micro	$\times 10^{-6}$
n	nano	$\times 10^{-9}$

Answering Calculation Questions

If you want to be confident in answering calculation questions; work through them methodically! Practice doing calculations with this simple four step process and you are much less likely to make mistakes... (and if you do make mistakes it'll be much easier for you to spot them and correct them!)

1. Identify all the data you have been given, and what you are being asked to calculate. Check the units and convert if necessary.

2. Select the equation, either one that you've memorised using this book, or that you are given in the formula sheet. Rearrange it if necessary, write it out!

3. Next rewrite the equation with the numbers instead of the terms, (you could get a mark just for this!)

4. Enter the whole sum into your calculator, check it, and check the units on your answer are coherent with what you've entered.

Density

$$\rho = \frac{m}{V}$$

$$density\ (kg/m^3) = \frac{mass\ (kg)}{volume\ (m^3)}$$

Pretty straightforward one to start with, density is how much matter there is in a certain space, it's mass per unit of volume, or kilograms per cubic metre. Most GCSEs have a required practical all about density, so that will be a common context for this equation. Also you'll see it's really useful later in Physics! And just so we're sure, that's not a P it's a Greek letter, "rho".

1. Calculate the density of a cube of expanded polystyrene with a mass of 0.5kg and a volume of $0.02m^3$.

$25kg/m^3$

2. Calculate the mass of a tipper truck loaded with coal. Coal has a density of around $900kg/m^3$ and a typical tipper truck has a volume of $10m^3$.

9 000kg (9t)

3. Calculate the Volume of container needed to store 4kg of olive oil for transportation. The density of olive oil $800kg/m^3$. Give your answer in cm^3.

$500cm^3$

Speed and Velocity

$$s = vt$$

distance travelled (m) = speed (m/s) × time (s)

Good old speed equals distance over time. Lots of Physics requires this definition, so get it right! A good one for cutting your teeth and for understanding how units work. Speed has units metres per second, which should remind you distance divided by time. Thinking like that should help you ensure you get your units conversions right.

Also I know it's strange at first, but we use v for speed, or velocity, and s for distance, or displacement. The s refers to space! (NOT speed!)

1. Calculate the average speed of a runner who completes the 100m event in 10s.

    10m/s

2. Calculate the distance that sound travels in 2s, given that sound has a speed of 343m/s in dry air and at room temperature.

    686m

3. Calculate the time taken to cover the 300km in a fast jet travelling at 600m/s.

    500s (8 mins 20s)

Acceleration

$$a = \frac{\Delta v}{t}$$

$$acceleration\ (m/s^2) = \frac{change\ in\ velocity\ (m/s)}{time\ (s)}$$

Acceleration is a rate of change of velocity (or change of speed.) Anything divided by time is a rate. Sometimes you'll see v-u instead of the Δv, but I prefer the little triangle, which is a Greek letter "delta" which we use in physics to mean "change in".

1. Calculate the acceleration of a toy car which reaches a top speed of 15m/s in 6s from a standing start.

$$2.5m/s^2$$

2. Calculate the time taken for a rollercoaster car to reach a top speed of 20m/s at an acceleration of $5m/s^2$.

$$4s$$

3. Calculate the final speed of a train which accelerates uniformly at a rate of $0.5m/s^2$ for 2 minutes.

$$60m/s$$

Kinetic Energy

$$E_k = \frac{1}{2}mv^2$$

kinetic energy (J)
$$= 0.5 \times mass\ (kg)$$
$$\times speed^2\ (m/s)$$

The kinetic energy store is that energy which is associated with an object that is moving. It can be tricky to rearrange, especially when making v the subject, so I suggest that you just remember:

$$v = \sqrt{\frac{2E_k}{m}}$$

That will save you the stress in the exam. This is an especially useful equation for energy analysis questions, which can be very tricky indeed, but really is just making one type of energy equal to another.

1. Calculate the kinetic energy of a 0.1kg ball moving from a tennis racquet at a speed of 50m/s.

125J

2. Calculate the velocity of a 2t (2 000kg) car moving with 900kJ (900 000J) of kinetic energy.

30m/s

3. Scientists measured the impact energy of a meteor at 2×10^{10}J and an impact velocity of 10km/s. Calculate the mass of the meteor.

400kg

Newton's Second Law

$$\Sigma F = ma$$

resultant force (N)
$= mass$ (kg)
$\times acceleration$ (m/s^2)

A useful equation to remember because both Newton's first and second laws are contained within it. In practice this equation allows you to work out the acceleration for a given mass, for a given force. Be careful though, because they may give you several forces, in which case you'll have to work out the net force, or resultant force before you use it. That's what the Greek letter "sigma" (the funny looking E before the F for force) means; *sum of, net or resultant.*

1. Calculate the magnitude of the resultant force which acts on a 2kg mass to cause an acceleration of 15m/s².

30N

2. Calculate the acceleration of a 500kg motorbike when a 6kN (6000N) resultant force acts on it.

12m/s²

3. An unmanned space craft main engine delivers 1.5kN of thrust, when fired in micro gravity orbit this gives an acceleration of 5m/s². Calculate the mass of the space craft.

300kg

Momentum

$$p = mv$$

$momentum\ (kgm/s) = mass(kg) \times velocity\ (m/s)$

Momentum is a tricky one to understand, at first it's
not immediately obvious why we need it as a
quantity, but imagine the difference between trying
to stop a lorry or a bicycle if they are travelling at the
same speed! Then the idea of momentum should
make sense. Or otherwise you can just treat it as
another quantity, the product of mass and velocity.
It has units as you would expect; kilograms times
metres per second. There are some tricky questions
using this formula, applying the law of conservation
of momentum, involving either collisions or
explosions!

1. Calculate the momentum of a 100kg rugby player running at 5m/s.

500kgm/s

2. Calculate the velocity of a 0.5kg trolley which has a momentum of 2kgm/s.

4m/s

3. Calculate the mass of a car travelling at 15m/s with a momentum of 22 500 kgm/s. Give your answer in tonnes.

1.5t

Work Done

$$W = F\Delta s$$

work done (J) = force (N) × distance (m)

Work done is the same physical quantity as energy. Specifically this is energy transferred by doing mechanical work, so by forces. Remember in the equation we use an *s* for a reason; *s* stands for displacement, which is a vector, so direction matters. In other words the distance that the object has moved must be along the line of action of the force. They may try and trip you up with a force at an angle, and you'd need to work out the component of that force in the direction of the displacement.

1. Calculate the work done by lifting a 10N weight through a height of 1.5m.

15J

2. Calculate the distance moved by a hydraulic press which uses a 100N of force and expends 200J in doing so.

2m

3. Calculate the average force exerted on an object which has been moved through a distance of 2km if 3MJ of energy has been transferred to it.

1500N

Power

$$P = \frac{W}{t}$$

$$power\ (W) = \frac{work\ done\ (J)}{time\ (s)}$$

Power is the rate of energy transfer. It has units Watts, (if you ever find yourself asking "what is the unit of power?") A rate is anything divided by time, i.e. anything per second. So in this case a Watt is a Joule per second. There are loads of reasons they could ask you to calculate or use the power equation, so it's a really useful one to know.

1. Calculate the power of a heater which transfers 7.2MJ (7 200 000) to a room when it is left on for an hour (3600s).

2 000W

2. Calculate the time taken to do 500J of mechanical work by a 50W motor.

10s

3. Calculate the energy transferred to the water in boiling a 1.5kW kettle for 3mins.

270 000J

Hooke's Law

$$F = k\Delta x$$

force (N) = spring constant (N/m)
× extension (m)

This is one of the simplest of proportional laws and is usually applied to the stretching of springs, but it could be any elastic material. This equation simply states that force is proportional to extension. So a graph of force on the y axis and extension on the x gives a straight line through the origin with the spring constant as its gradient. They like to probe your understanding of gradients with this one, and remember that the delta, (the triangle) is a significant one; we're talking about extension, i.e. a change in length not a length.

1. Calculate the load force on a spring which has been extended by 0.3m and has a stiffness of 25N/m.

7.5N

2. Calculate the stiffness of the spring in a toy gun which compresses 5cm (0.05m) under a 5N force.

100N/m

3. Calculate the extension of a pen spring with a stiffness of 100N/m if a 1.5N force is applied to it. Give your answer in cm.

1.5cm

Weight and Mass

$$W = mg$$

weight (N) = mass (kg) × g (N/kg)

This is really a straightforward definition. The difference between weight, which is a force due to gravity, and mass, which is a measure of how difficult something is to accelerate. But this is something that you will need to get right because both mass and weight are used in other calculations! Little g is gravitational field strength (or gravitational acceleration), most specs require you to remember that g = 10N/kg, but careful because I've seen GCSEs give it as 9.8N/kg or even 9.81N/kg.

1. Calculate the weight of a 60kg person on the moon. Use 1.7N/kg as the moon's gravitational field strength.

35N

2. On the International Space Station (ISS) gravitational field strength is approximately 3×10^{-3}N/kg. The force of gravity on the space station is 1500N, calculate the mass of the ISS.

500 000kg

3. Using a precise digital force-meter a mass of 60g is weighed. The scale reads 0.588N. What is the gravitational field strength on Earth?

9.8N/kg

Gravitational Potential Energy

$$E_p = mgh$$

potential energy (J)
= mass (kg) × g (N/kg)
× height (m)

"Energy due to being raised in a gravitational field."
But most of the time using this will be simpler than
that idea! However look out for using this equation
for energy analysis, i.e. making one type of energy
equal to another so that we can calculate an
unknown quantity. It is useful to remember *mg* is
equal to a force, as in the equation *W=mg*, so this
equation is really very similar to the work done
equation.

1. Calculate the gravitational energy gained by a plate being placed on a shelf 1.5m metres from the ground. Assume that g=10N/kg and that the plate has a mass of 0.3kg.

4.5J

2. Calculate the mass of an object given 200J of gravitational potential energy when it is placed on a house roof 5m above the ground. Assume g=10N/kg.

4kg

3. Calculate the height that a 1 tonne car would reach if it were fired straight up gaining 1MJ of gravitational energy. Assume g=10N/kg.

100m

Pressure on a Surface

$$P = \frac{F}{A}$$

$$pressure\ (Pa) = \frac{force\ (N)}{area\ (m^2)}$$

A really useful equation for working out the effect of forces on surfaces. Remember to use the force, or component of the force at right angles to the surface. But also this is useful for explaining and making calculations with hydraulic systems. There's a short cut with hydraulics though, they multiply forces in the ratio of the piston areas.

1. Calculate the Pressure exerted by an elephant which has a weight of 60kN (60 000N) and total foot surface area of 0.6m^2.

100 000Pa

2. Calculate the area of the head of a nail which is struck with 50N of force and applies a pressure of 5MPa (5 000 000Pa).

1×10^{-5}m^2

3. Calculate the force produced by a hydraulic press piston with an area of 2cm^2 and a pressure of 1MPa.

20 000N

Moments

$$M = Fd$$

moment (Nm) = force (N) × distance (m)

The moment of a force is its turning effect. Sometimes we call this its *torque*. It's how much a force acts to turn something around a pivot. This will usually be used in calculations using the principle of moments which states; "if something is balanced around a pivot then the sum of the clockwise moments equals the sum of the anticlockwise moments". It is also really useful for explaining and calculating with levers, which are force multipliers. Remember to use the perpendicular distance to the pivot from the line of action of the force.

1. Calculate the moment acting around the pivot in a pair of scissors when a force of 5N acts 0.06m from the pivot.

0.3Nm

2. Calculate the distance from the centre of a see-saw that a large gentleman weighing 1000N would have to sit to balance a small child producing a moment of 500Nm.

0.5m

3. Calculate the force on one side of a motor block which produces a 0.003Nm and has a length from the pivot of 2cm. Assume all forces are at right angles and continuous.

0.15N

Current

$$Q = It$$

charge flow (C) = current (A) × time(s)

This is probably the first thing that you should get straight about electricity. This equation defines what a current is. A current is a rate of flow of charge, which you'll see if you rearrange for current:

$$I = \frac{Q}{t}$$

But this equation is also very useful for working out the total charge passed a point if we know the current and how long it's been flowing. That unit C for charge is a Coulomb, in case you ever need to say it!

1. Calculate the charge flowing past a point if a 2A current runs for 20s.

   40C

2. Calculate the current if 600C of charge flows for 1200s.

   0.5A

3. Calculate the time for 30mC charge to flow through a bulb at a current of 3A.

   0.01s

Ohm's Law

$$V = IR$$

potential difference (V)
$$= current\ (A) \times resistance\,(\Omega)$$

Ohm's Law, perhaps the most commonly used equation of the lot, and it's so simple and so elegant! Voltage and current are proportional, and the constant of proportionality is the resistance. There is rarely an electricity question that goes by without you needing to use or make reference to this equation. It's also really very useful for circuit analysis questions!

1. Calculate the potential difference that causes a 0.5A current to flow through a 10Ω resistor.

5V

2. Calculate the current when a 12V power pack is connected across a 4Ω bulb.

3A

3. Calculate the resistance of a fixed resistor if a 3mA current is measured when it is connected to a 6V battery.

2 000Ω (2k Ω)

Potential Difference

$$E = QV$$

energy transferred (J)
= charge (C)
× potential difference (V)

This equation is really useful for defining what a potential difference is. Rearrange it for potential difference and you get energy per unit charge. Which makes a lot of sense really:

$$V = \frac{E}{Q}$$

The potential difference is how much energy is given to the charge! It's the reason for the charge to move and it's the reason that the charge can do electrical work in the components!

1. Calculate the energy dissipated by a 12V bulb when 400C of charge has flowed through it.

4800J

2. Calculate the potential difference if 30J is supplied to 6C of charge.

5V

3. A kettle transfers 115kJ of energy to boil a cup of water. Calculate the charge which has flowed through its heating element. Assume it is connected to mains electricity (230V).

500C

Electrical Power

$$P = IV$$

power (W) = current (A)
× potential difference (V)

Quite often you'll be asked to comment on the
brightness of bulbs, and in previous years it was
probably enough to think of the brightness as being
caused by the current, so more current, brighter
bulb. Whilst that is not wrong, it's not the full
picture. Brightness depends on the power, the rate
of transfer of energy. And electrical power is the
product of the current and the voltage. A really
useful equation in electricity topics.

1. Calculate the power output of a 12V heater, given an ammeter connected in series with it reads 4A.

48W

2. Calculate the potential difference supplied to a motor which is running at a power of 100W if the current running through it is 5A.

20V

3. Calculate the current through the heating element for a 2.3kW kettle connected to the mains electricity supply.

10A

Power Loss

$$P = I^2 R$$

power loss (W) = current^2 (A) × resistance (Ω)

This is a derived equation made by replacing the *V* in *P=IV* with *IR* from Ohm's law. Essentially this is just another way of calculating power. But it also lets us explain how we get much less power loss if we can keep the current to a minimum, so expect to see it in this context. Often they use this equation to justify the use of transformers in the national grid, these reduce the power loss and make the whole thing more efficient. As you can see, power is proportional to current squared! This means double the current, four times the power.

1. Calculate the power dissipated as a 2A current flows through a 10Ω resistor.

40W

2. Calculate the resistance of a 100W bulb which has a 5A current flowing through it.

4Ω

3. Calculate the current through a section of overhead power cables which are transmitting 1GW of power and have a resistance of 1kΩ.

1 000A (1kA)

Energy, Power and Time

$$\Delta E = Pt$$

$energy\ transferred\ (J, kWh)$
$\qquad = power\ (W, kW) \times time\ (s, h)$

You've already come across this definition of energy transferred and power before, and the difference between work done and energy transferred is a pretty academic one. But notice a subtle difference in the units here. This time we introduce the much larger unit of energy, the kilo-watt-hour. As this is the unit in which we pay for electricity in homes and industries.

1. Calculate the energy transferred 2kW heater runs for 200hours over the course of a winter. Give your answer in kWh.

400kWh

2. Calculate the power in Watts that a TV uses if it transfers 100 000J in 200s.

500W

3. An electric car is plugged into a 10kW charging station. The owner uses 20kWh of energy to charge it. Calculate the time in hours for which it was charging.

2hours

Wave Speed

$$v = f\lambda$$

wave speed (m/s)
= frequency (Hz)
× wavelength (m)

Simply put this states that frequency and wavelength are inversely proportional to one another, and the constant of that proportionality is the wave speed. Remember that the speed of a wave is determined by the medium that it is travelling in, and is fixed in that medium, regardless of, frequency, wavelength, amplitude or anything else. Remember that sometimes you might need to get a frequency from a time period, which is easy as if time period is in seconds, and a Hertz is like saying "per second" then:

$$f = \frac{1}{T} \quad \text{and} \quad T = \frac{1}{f}$$

1. A student measures waves on a slinky. The frequency was 2Hz and wavelength of 2m. Calculate the wave speed.

4m/s

2. Orange light has a wavelength of 6×10^{-7}m and a wave speed of 3×10^{8}m/s. Calculate its frequency.

5×10^{14}Hz

3. Waves on a beach travel at 3m/s and there is one every ten seconds. Calculate the wavelength.

30m

Efficiency

$$E_f = \frac{\Delta E_u}{\Delta E_T}$$

$$Efficiency = \frac{useful\ output\ energy\ transfer\ (J)}{input\ energy\ transfer\ (J)}$$

Efficiency is defined as the ratio of the energy that is transferred usefully to the total which is transferred. There is always going to be a certain proportion of energy which is wasted, by heating the surroundings, (this is a fundamental law in fact!) This is where all the stuff in maths where you learn about the equivalency of fractions, decimals and percentages come in handy! You can also calculate efficiency if you are given input power and useful power transfer, it's just the same maths skills. Just make sure you get useful and waste the right way around!

1. A compact filament bulb transfers 18J of every 20J of electrical energy it is supplied into light. Calculate its efficiency.

0.9 (90%)

2. Calculate the gravitational energy store of a motor lifting a weight which is 30% efficient. The motor does 600J of electrical working in total.

180J

3. Calculate the useful energy output of a battery which wastes 25% of its chemical energy store when running. When fully charged it has a store of 10kJ.

7.5kJ (7 500J)

Congratulations

That's all the equations you need to remember for your exams. Next are the equations that you need to be able to select and know how to use.

But you aren't done with the previous pages, you'll need to go over them a few times so that they really stick in your mind.

Maybe go through the equations again and draw a little picture which is linked to that topic, for example a spring on Hooke's Law. Memory tends to be more effective when linked to visuals in this way.

Also, check that you can rearrange them in your head, and maybe have a go at the hardest question on each page again.

Then, make sure you review this one last time on the morning of the exam so that each equation is fresh in your mind. Note down any that you are likely to forget as soon as you start your paper!

Next...

These are the equations that you just need to know how to use. They tend to be some of the more tricky concepts in GCSE.

They are often equations that do not fit the standard three quantity proportional relationship. That makes them a little harder to rearrange at times as you'll need to move more than one quantity in the right order.

Many students find it easier to input the numbers before re-arranging, then just simplify until they have their answer. This is good because you can often get a mark for just getting the right data in the right place in the right equation! Another reason to always show your working.

Whatever you do though, focus on the same skills; identify the data, convert to standard units, select the equation, input, rearrange, calculate and check.

Specific Heat Capacity

$$\Delta E = mc\Delta T$$

*change in thermal energy (J) = mass (kg) ×
specific heat capacity (J/kg°C) ×
change in temperature (°C)*

All materials have a specific heat capacity, it's like saying how much thermal energy they store for each kilogram, for each degree Celsius. This equation will usually be used in connection with experiments to do with measuring the specific heat capacity of a material, but it could also be used to explain the thermal behaviour of a substance, or even to justify a choice of material based on its thermal properties. Remember they could give you temperatures in degrees Kelvin, and that each one degree Kelvin is equal to one degree Celsius. They just have a different zero, 0K = -273°C. Notice also the important deltas (Δ), so look out for things like "starting temperature" or hidden data like "heated until it boils".

1. Calculate the energy required to increase 0.5kg of water by 10°C. The specific heat capacity of water is 4200J/kg°C.

21 000J (21kJ)

2. Calculate the temperature rise of 10kg an alloy which has a specific heat capacity of 900J/kg°C when its thermal energy store increases by 18 000J.

2°C

3. A student conducts a practical to measure the specific heat capacity of copper. Their measurements are:
energy = 8kJ, mass = 1kg,
starting temperature = 30°C,
final temperature = 50°C.

400 J/kg°C

Specific Latent Heat

$$E = mL$$

thermal energy for a change in state (J) = mass (kg) × specific latent heat (J/kg)

This is amazing really, it's the idea that during a change of state the thermal energy input to a substance doesn't increase the temperature of a material. It's the strongest evidence for the kinetic theory of matter; all substances are made of particles with kinetic energy and are attracted to each other with intermolecular forces. The energy is involved in making or breaking those forces during a change of state. Be careful because the values are different for solid-liquid changes and for liquid-gas changes. It doesn't matter which direction the change is happening: solid-liquid we call fusion, and liquid-gas we call vaporisation.

1. Calculate the energy required to melt 2kg of ice. The specific latent heat of fusion of water is 334 000J/kg.

668 000J

2. Calculate the mass of nitrogen that would be evaporated by an energy change of 99 500J. The specific latent heat of vaporisation of nitrogen is 199 000J/kg.

0.5kg

3. A 1g mass of carbon dioxide condenses, in doing so the surroundings' thermal energy store gains 574J. Calculate the specific latent heat of vaporisation for carbon dioxide.

574 000J/kg

Electrical Energy

$$E = VIt$$

electrical energy (J)
$\qquad = potential\ difference\ (V)$
$\qquad \times current\ (A) \times time\ (s)$

This equation only appears in the Edexcel
specification, but it's actually a pretty useful equation
for all specs to know and use. Essentially it states
that energy is power times time, they've just subbed
in the equation for electrical power which is
potential difference times current to give one
equation for electrical energy transferred. This will
be really useful for energy analysis and for the
specific heat capacity practical that appears in many
GCSE specifications.

1. Calculate the energy transferred by a 10V immersion heater which has a current of 4A and is switched on for 200s.

8000J

2. Calculate the time for which a 6V battery operated fan is switched on for, given that it draws a current of 0.4A and transfers 300J of energy from the battery.

125s

3. A motor runs for 10 minutes from a car's 12V power supply, during which time it transfers 1440J of energy. Calculate the current it draws.

0.2A

Boyle's Law

$$PV = k$$

pressure (Pa) × volume (m³) = constant

Boyle's Law is the inverse proportionality of pressure and volume for a fixed mass of gas and at a constant temperature. They are going to want you to do calculations with it so it won't be enough to say, "higher pressure, lower volume." You need to appreciate that double the pressure, halve the volume. For that reason I prefer at times to write $P \propto \frac{1}{V}$ or even:

$$P_1 V_1 = P_2 V_2$$

This form is especially useful if they give you a pressure and volume initially, and then tell you a new volume or pressure and ask you to work out the other one!

1. The volume of a fixed mass of gas is 50m^3. The pressure inside the balloon halves, but the temperature remains constant. Calculate the new volume of the balloon.

$$100m^3$$

2. A sealed container of nitrogen a volume of 100cm^3 at a pressure of 100kPa. It is compressed under a pressure of 400kPa. Calculate the new volume of the gas.

$$25cm^3$$

3. In one estimate the pressure inside the sun is 2.5×10^{14}Pa. The volume of the sun is approximately 1×10^{27}m^3. Calculate the pressure in its expected red giant phase if it were to expand to 1×10^{36}m^3 in its expected red giant phase.

$$250\ 000Pa$$

Pressure and Depth

$$P = h\rho g$$

$pressure\ (Pa) = height\ (m)$
$\times density\ (kg/m^3)$
$\times g\ (N/kg)$

Most usually this will be used to calculate a pressure
in a column of liquid, for example at a depth in
water. But it can also be used to explain the force
upthrust which is caused by the slightly higher
pressure underneath an object compared to above.
Remember once more that there is the value g, for
gravitational field strength, which you should
remember is 10N/kg.

1. Calculate the pressure at the bottom of a 3m swimming pool. The density of water is 1 000kg/m^3 and assume g=10N/kg.

   30 000Pa

2. The pressure at the bottom of a well of crude oil is 8 000 000Pa. Calculate the depth of the well given that the density of the crude oil is 800kg/m^3 and the gravitational field strength on earth is 10N/kg.

   1 000m

3. A pressure sensor at the base of a 20cm column of liquid methane reads 1kPa Calculate the density of liquid methane. Assume g=10N/kg.

   500kg/m^3

Equation of Uniform Acceleration

$$v^2 = u^2 + 2as$$

final velocity² (m/s) = initial velocity² (m/s) + 2 × acceleration (m/s²) × distance (m)

In many GCSEs now this is the only equation of motion that you'll need to use and tends to be used in the context of stopping distances in cars. Look out for a statement like "an object accelerates uniformly" to give you a clue to use it. Uniform acceleration means that the acceleration is constant. Look out for hidden data like, "from rest", or "to a stop". It can be a tricky one to rearrange, so many students find it easier to input all the data that they know then simplify step by step until they arrive at their final answer. Many students also forget the squared, or the root when rearranging, so look out for that. In any case find out which way works for you by having a go at these questions.

1. Calculate the final velocity of a train which accelerates uniformly from rest over a distance of 2 500m at a rate of 0.5m/s^2.

50m/s

2. Calculate the distance covered by a car which accelerates from an initial velocity of 10m/s to 20m/s at a rate of 2.5m/s^2.

60m

3. Calculate the acceleration of a sprinter who accelerates from zero to 10m/s over a distance of 25m.

2m/s^2

Other Equations of Uniform Acceleration

$$v = u + at$$

$$s = \frac{1}{2}(u + v)t$$

$$s = ut + \frac{1}{2}at^2$$

s = distance (m)   t = time (s)   u = initial velocity (m/s)
v = final velocity (m/s)   a = acceleration (m/s²)

Eduqas have included all the three other equations of motion, but they are worth knowing, especially if you are interested in A Level Physics. They can also be a useful shortcut at times! Make sure you know what all the algebra means, and then just think, "which three quantities do I know, and which one thing am I trying to find out?" Plug the numbers in, simplify, rearrange and go!

1. Calculate the final velocity of a car which accelerates at 0.5m/s^2 for 10 seconds from an initial velocity of 25m/s to overtake a heavy good vehicle.

30m/s

2. Calculate the distance travelled by a motorbike which slows from 20m/s to a stop at a set of traffic lights in a time of 5s.

50m

3. A train is travelling at 40m/s in a tunnel before accelerating at a rate of 0.2m/s^2 for 1 minute. Calculate the distance the train travels during this time.

2760m

Elastic Strain Energy

$$E_{el} = \frac{1}{2} k \Delta x^2$$

elastic strain energy (J) = 0.5 ×
spring constant (N/m) × exension^2 (m)

This equation is really useful for energy analysis as
you might imagine. It is likely to be used in
conjunction with Hooke's Law to first calculate a
spring constant, then use it to calculate an energy.
This energy could then be used to calculate a speed
using the kinetic energy equation, or maybe a height
using gravitational potential energy equation. It also
is an expression of the fact that the area under a
force-extension graph is equivalent to the energy
stored in the spring.

1. Calculate the elastic strain energy in slinky which is extended by 5m and has a spring constant of 0.5N/m.

6.25J

2. Calculate the extension of a spring with a spring constant of 20N/m and which has 250J in its elastic potential energy store.

5m

3. Calculate the spring constant of an elastic band which stores 1J of elastic strain energy when it stretches by 10cm. Give your answer in N/m.

200N/m

Magnification

$$M = \frac{h_i}{h_o}$$

$$magnification = \frac{image\ height}{object\ height}$$

Only the AQA triple science specification requires you to use this equation, but they all include the lenses and the idea of comparing images, so it's an idea worth knowing about. It's pretty simple anyway, it's just like a scale factor in maths. Magnification is how many times bigger the image is than the object; simple. I haven't given units as there are no units for magnification as it's a ratio. Just make sure that the unit of image height is the same as the unit for object height.

1. Calculate the magnification of a microscope that creates an image 4mm high of an object which is 0.1mm high.

40

2. Calculate the height of the image created of a 20m tall tree on the retina of an eye if the magnification is 0.0005.

0.01m

3. Large format cameras have sensors which are 15cm tall and are used to take photographs of buildings and landscapes with little lens distortion. Calculate the maximum height of building that can be photographed using a lens and sensor combination which creates a magnification of 0.0025.

60m

the Motor Effect

$$F = BIl$$

force (N) = magnetic field stength (T)
× current (A) × length (m)

This equation allows you to calculate the force on a
current carrying conductor in a magnetic field. The
quantity B represents the strength of that field, or as
we often say the magnetic flux density. You can
remember it as that quantity measured in Tesla (T).
Flux is a difficult idea, but I guess it is enough for
you at GCSE just to think of it as being the lines in a
magnetic field drawing, if there are more of them in
a given area then there will be a stronger field there,
so a higher magnetic flux density. Remember that
the length will be the length of the wire *in the
magnetic field*. Look out for this one in questions
about the motor effect, and make sure you can rearrange it and use it accurately.

1. Calculate the Force on a 0.05m wire carrying a current of 3A in a 0.2T field.

    0.03N

2. Calculate the length of wire needed to produce a force of 6N in a 0.5T field if it has a current of 10A.

    1.2m

3. The Earth's magnetic field strength is approximately 50μT. Calculate the current running through a 60cm length of wire if a 15mN force is measured on it.

    500A

the Transformer Equation

$$\frac{V_p}{V_s} = \frac{N_p}{N_s}$$

$$\frac{potential\ difference\ across\ primary\ coil\ (V)}{potential\ difference\ across\ secondary\ coil\ (V)}$$
$$= \frac{number\ of\ turns\ in\ primary\ coil}{number\ of\ turns\ in\ secondary\ coil}$$

Transformers transform voltages. Whether they step-up the voltage, or step it down depends upon the ratio of the turns on the primary coil to the turns on the secondary. Honestly, this is really easy to use. Write out the formula, then fill in the three numbers you know and use the last one to make the two fractions equal! It's just all ratios really.

1. A transformer has a ratio of turns of 1:4 from primary coil to secondary coil. The potential difference across the primary coils is 20V. Calculate the potential difference across the secondary coil.

80V

2. Calculate the number of turns needed on the secondary coil for a step down transformer to transform a 20V supply voltage to a 5V output voltage. The primary coil has 240 turns.

60 turns

3. Calculate the voltage across the primary coil for a transformer which steps up the potential difference to 400kV for transmission in the national grid. The transformer has 10 000 turns on its secondary coil and 500 on the primary.

20kV (20 000V)

the Transformer Power Equation

$$V_p I_p = V_s I_s$$

*potential difference across primary coil (V) ×
current in primary coil (A) =
potential difference across secondary coil (V) ×
current in secondary coil (A)*

In an ideal transformer the power input is the same as the power output. So this allows us to calculate the current or voltage output if we know the current and voltage input. So this equation simply states that the electrical power in is equal to the electrical power out. Essentially though, once again, you are going to be given three out of these four values and work out the fourth. Practice doing that and also practice checking your answer in case you made an error in rearranging.

1. Calculate the current output of a transformer which has a potential difference across the primary coil of 30V and a potential difference across the secondary coil of 300V. The current in the primary coil is 10A.

    1A

2. Calculate the potential difference across the secondary coil of a step down transformer which has a primary current of 3A and a secondary current of 6A. The potential difference across the primary coil is 230V.

    115V

3. The transformer in a substation has a potential difference across the primary coil of 400kV and a current through the primary coil of 1kA. Calculate the current output if the output potential difference is 20kV.

    20kA

Congratulations

That's the end of all the equations that you need to know and know how to use, but you aren't done with this book yet!

Practice makes perfect, by practicing these questions again, and by applying the skills that you have learned from this book to other questions, you'll make yourself fluent in answering the calculation questions in your exam.

By being more confident with the calculations you're going to save yourself time so that you can really think about those harder questions in the exam.

Once you are really confident with the easier calculations make sure you practice some of the hardest calculations that you could be asked to do at GCSE level.

What's next?

Really hard calculations… but what makes them hard?

It's that there isn't one equation that you are given, or are expected to remember, that will allow you to complete the calculation. So you have to do two calculations to reach the final answer.

These types of question are usually worth four or more marks, so look out for the number of marks to help you recognise them.

It will be worth thinking, "what *can* I calculate with the data I'm given?" That may get you part way to solving the problem, and will probably be worth some of the marks anyway.

As before, I'll give you the answer but no working, so you know what you're aiming for, and then if you really struggle I'll put a page of hints after them all, to tell you the two equations you should be using.

1. A measuring cylinder is placed on a scale which is reset to read 0g. It is then filled with a liquid to the 100cm^3 mark, the scale now reads 90.0g. A student then measures the height of the column of liquid as 20.0cm, before inserting a pressure sensor to the bottom of the cylinder. Predict what the pressure will be at the base of the column of liquid.

1800Pa

2. A constant force of 5N is applied to a toy rocket of 4g over a distance of 10cm. Calculate the speed of the bolt as it leaves the launcher. Ignore the effects of friction and air resistance. Give your answer to 3 significant figures.

15.8m/s

3. Two cars are involved in a head on collision. The masses of the two cars are shown on the diagram. The car which is driving east had a device which records its speed and so was able to report to the police a speed of 25m/s, which is the speed limit on the road. After the collision the two cars moved as one mass toward the west with a combined speed of 5m/s. Conclude whether the west bound car was speeding.

west   east

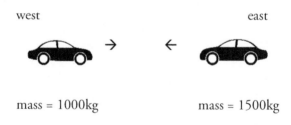

mass = 1000kg   mass = 1500kg

No, it was also travelling at 25m/s.

4. A heavy duty construction crane has a maximum lifting capacity of 42 tonnes at its maximum radius of 100m. Calculate the moment about the central column.

1 tonne = 1000kg

42 000 000Nm

5. A student is conducting a practical by adding slotted masses to a spring. They notice that the spring extends proportionally up to a force of 10N when the extension is 20cm. Calculate the energy stored in the spring when 10N weight is hanging from it.

1J

6. A potential difference of 20V is connected across a resistance of 50Ω. Calculate the charge through the resistor if it is left connected for a 10 hours.

14 400C

7. A student places some ice cubes in a sealed plastic bag are placed into a beaker of water. The plastic bag is removed once all of the ice is melted. The mass of water in the beaker, mass of ice, starting temperature of water and final temperature of the water are all measured and recorded in the table below. The student also looks up a value for the specific heat capacity of water. Calculate the specific latent heat of fusion for water using the student's results.

mass of water	180g
mass of ice	30g
starting temperature of water	35°C
final temperature of water	20°C
specific heat capacity of water	4200J/kg°C

378 000J/kg

8. A balloon containing 500g of air with a volume of 0.4m^3 is submerged underwater to a depth of 10m where the pressure is double atmospheric pressure. Calculate the density of the air in the submerged balloon.

2.5kg/m^3

9. A 5cm length wire with a mass of 0.035g is held in a 0.1T magnetic field. It is connected to a power pack, which is then switched on. Immediately a 2A current flows through the wire. Calculate the initial acceleration of the wire. You can ignore the weight of the wire.

$286m/s^2$

10. A step down transformer is used to reduce 230V mains voltage to power a laptop. It has a primary coil with 900 turns and a secondary coil of 75. It draws a current from the mains of 0.30A. Calculate the current supplied to the laptop.

3.6A

Hints

1. $\rho = \dfrac{m}{V}$ $P = h\rho g$

2. $W = F\Delta s$ $E_k = \dfrac{1}{2}mv^2$ or
   $\Sigma F = ma$ $v^2 = u^2 + 2as$

3. $p = mv$ and Law of Conservation of
   Momentum, i.e. momentum before =
   momentum after

4. $W = mg$ $M = Fd$

5. $F = k\Delta x$ $E_{el} = \dfrac{1}{2}k\Delta x^2$

6. $V = IR$ $Q = It$

7. $\Delta E = mc\Delta T$ $E = mL$

8. $PV = k$ $\rho = \dfrac{m}{V}$

9. $F = BIl$ $\Sigma F = ma$

10. $\dfrac{V_p}{V_s} = \dfrac{N_p}{N_s}$ $V_p I_p = V_s I_s$

about GorillaPhysics

GorillaPhysics is a YouTube channel and website created entirely by Kit Betts-Masters, a Head of Physics at a secondary school in England.

GorillaPhysics has tutorial videos for all topics in GCSE and A Level Physics, including practical demonstrations, example calculations and full explanations of past paper questions. There are also lots of study tips, advice on preparing for exams and on exam technique. Come on over to the channel and subscribe!

GorillaPhysics.com has the videos mapped out by topic, and is being developed to include tutorial pages and useful information and links for both teachers and students.

I really hope you find this book useful, and regardless of how you got it, I'm glad you have it! Perhaps drop by my YouTube channel and say thanks, or better yet, tell your friends, siblings or teachers that you found it useful and point them in the direction to get it!

I ask that you please don't send each other people copies of the eBook, but go through the many ways to download this officially, or better yet, buy a paperback to keep in your pocket!

If you are a teacher, or head of subject, and intend on giving the book to entire classes or years, then please go ahead and find the book on TES resources by *kitbm* and pay for a site licence, it'll not be very expensive! I'll also include a word document so you can take out the equations which do not apply to your syllabus.

I'd welcome any and all feedback on this book and on my channel so please do drop by and leave a comment on YouTube, or a review on either Amazon, TES resources or Smashwords.

Please help me be more useful to more people by spreading the word about GorillaPhysics. Thanks!!!

Printed in Great Britain
by Amazon

48176311R00058